ISHMAEL MASK

PRAISE FOR *ISHMAEL MASK*

The poet must have a Nietzschean ambition to see beyond the mirror, beyond the absurd mask of consciousness. *Ishmael Mask* speaks to this primitive damage, the inescapable futility underlying life and depicted by literary fiction. Consider "The Green Hat" sequence, a masterpiece of metaphysical anxiety. The flickering periphery is a warning, and yet here are the poverties of memory, addiction, and imprisonment, recanted by Charles Kell in Melvillian drag. And yet, these obsessions—like Pierre's—under Kell's skillful pressure, offer surprising musical comforts. Tender, gothic, and wonderfully catastrophic, Kell's exhilarating poems flicker with both omen and mystery. Their dangers are sexy, lyrically precise, and elegiac. Their disquietude will leave you breathless.

— **Miguel Murphy**

Poetry is rarely so vividly an art of the face-to-face as it is in Charles Kell's *Ishmael Mask*: the faces of the dead, the faces in the mirror, the faces of the lover, blurred by presence and distance. These poems, shadowed by Melville and Kafka, are also a history of one poet's encounters with the inscrutable relentlessness of fate and the inevitable privacy of suffering. "One can draw loss, draw frost without anyone knowing," he writes. Yet knowing here becomes his reader's privilege, an unveiling slowly emerging through the voice of his haunting, indelible, lines.

—**Susan Stewart**

How does one hammer memory onto the page without nails or bullets? Charles Kell wails his own mnemonic siren through the literary specter of Herman Melville's *Pierre*, Kafka, etc., and we wail with him like a stone who can easily weep, but we don't. There is a touchless erection in this book and drowning and death and suicide and a "rat runs in small circles where the green hat used to lie" and may suggest life and pain and existential revisitations have cast shadows that are bigger than meadows. Perhaps in this collection Charles Kell is yelling from the top of his lungs, but all we could hear is wind and January or "black, red, green spiral of smoke." Or perhaps Kell and his poetry are a cellar we all wish we could descend into to grab mason jars of beauty and grace in times of existential hunger and famine.

—**Vi Khi Nao**

We Americans are all imaginary orphans, forever seeking a new name, a new carapace, and the further adventure. "Call me Ishmael" is thus a motto more proper to our republic, and more forward-looking, than "E Pluribus Unum." In *Ishmael Mask*, Charles Kell has parsed the fossil record of our orphancy in beautiful and unguarded detail; he has adventured much and withheld nothing. For those who come to poetry in search of a credible future, Kell will prove to be a true and unfailingly honest companion.

—**Donald Revell**

ISHMAEL MASK

CHARLES KELL

AUTUMN
HOUSE PRESS
Pittsburgh, PA

Cover and Book Design: Melissa Dias-Mandoly
Cover Art: Martin Kippenberger. *Untitled* (from the series *Self-portraits*), 1988. Oil on canvas. 240 x 200 cm. © Estate of Martin Kippenberger, Galerie Gisela Capitain, Cologne.
Author Photo: Carrie Kell

Library of Congress Cataloging-in-Publication Data

Names: Kell, Charles, author.
Title: Ishmael mask / Charles Kell.
Description: Pittsburgh, PA : Autumn House Press, [2023]
Identifiers: LCCN 2022046618 (print) | LCCN 2022046619 (ebook) | ISBN
   9781637680704 (paperback) | ISBN 9781637680711 (epub)
Subjects: LCGFT: Poetry.
Classification: LCC PS3611.E3884 I84 2023 (print) | LCC PS3611.E3884
   (ebook) | DDC 811/.6--dc23/eng/20220928
LC record available at https://lccn.loc.gov/2022046618
LC ebook record available at https://lccn.loc.gov/2022046619

Autumn House Press is a nonprofit corporation whose mission is the publication and promotion of poetry and other fine literature. The press gratefully acknowledges support from individual donors, public and private foundations, and government agencies. This book was supported, in part, by the Greater Pittsburgh Arts Council through its Allegheny Arts Revival Grant and the Pennsylvania Council on the Arts, a state agency funded by the Commonwealth of Pennsylvania.

TABLE OF CONTENTS

I.

II.

III.

IV.

for Miguel Murphy

I.

Tell me once more the story of that face, Pierre,—that mysterious, haunting face, which thou once told'st me, thou didst thrice vainly try to shun.

—Herman Melville, *Pierre; or, The Ambiguities*

VEIL

Who I spoke to when
I said barely a word,
staring in the dim mirror
while a fire blazed
in the dark next room.
Sick smell of soft moss
scraped from a trunk, doused
with turpentine.

Smoke hiding half of my face—

PERFUME

Last summer your skin tasted
of orange peel, lies

buried deep in your lungs.
Never more than two words: *that hurts*

or *like that*, *right there*. Every-
thing inside became unmoored—

the Stanley knife you stole
could barely break flesh,

the love letters we scrawled on cedar
panels. The fabulous taxidermy

you found in that shed buried
in a Windham forest, how you

slowly led me by the hand, pointed
at the lock you knew all along I would break.

How we sat under hulking antlers
drinking warm beer, whispering to each

other the books we would write.
Artemis, Lethe, you said.

Beaver, formaldehyde, sodium borate.
A fawn with tiny pins sticking from its eyes.

MONSIEUR MELVILLE

Make a fist of smoke then bray
at the stars. November is a paper wing.
Obelisk of moving water,
on the quay, a dangling spur.

All right, sir, are your papers in order?
Is it a nag or a whaler?
With legs like yours, sir, it would
be a sin to go for just a walk.

You are a machine. Your gaze
goes beyond the ball.
Two hundred pounds of sullen
flesh, fifty of corrosive muscle

mast-tied during a storm? Stripped
& lashed with a bullwhip? The truths—
insular, viscous. Ants bore into
the planks of the hull, brown flakes

dapple white paper. Ink-smudged.
Call him the guilty one—sparrows
in his eyes. The whole world right
where you stand, there isn't another.

ASP

Feel my shape—fossil
back from black ash

to a picture on the mantel.
Out of that zinc sheet

into a hot bubble. Out of steel
steps dripping white

paint, green skin tossed
off along the rail. Out of names,

nickel, ampersand. The marriage
of tongue to salt back to chilled

aluminum. You were catching
my breath for hours on end.

THE GREEN HAT

buried in slush,
alone, stranded on the side
of the street. It wasn't there
yesterday when snow
fell in blurred clumps.

It's large, yet lost children
sometimes wear grown-
up skin when they want
to act somber,
take on the world's debt.

Someone is waking from
a dream, *Where is my green hat?*
A face in a dark room,
another hangover,
burnt eel-black.

ISHMAEL MOSQUE

Men rub red pepper into my shoulders
& barefoot we shuffle
toward the wall past slabs
of meat covered in flies past chaat
stands & sheep sleepwalking
around Gadodia Market
look at this mostly straight white man
bent in supplication
as he approaches Sunehri Mosque
Shri Shiv Navgrah temple words
float in curtains of air
sweat drips down cheeks
then on to Chandni Chowk
among diesel & dung until
I reach for a piece of paratha
& dab my forehead
sprinkle a few drops on the man
in front of me

BUZZARDS

In the middle of Morrison's
field, slightly buzzed and not
caring if I call
or go back home.

Before the foreclosure
we sold what we could:
seeder, tiller, row-crop
cultivator, round baler.

I wouldn't take a dime for my work:
driving, cleaning, loading
what it takes two men
to move. I am labor—

I listened then carried.
I held the matches, the can
of gasoline, as Luke
threw the fire down.

Now, still and alone,
in the dark beginning
of an Ohio August night,
in the smoldering

grass, smelling fumes, sweat,
I wait for Luke to return
with the brown powder and Wild
Turkey, for the wish of two

years ago, when his father
was alive, when
there was a slight chance
he would still have a home.

DEAD LETTER OFFICE

Work papers bound in blue string;
table ink spills across

a slanted floor; keyholes rattle in the cold
New Bedford wind. Here is my mouth again.

Sweating barrel of an empty bottle.
Phlegm from a November catarrh.

Here is the *Scratching of Plague Years*.
Barbed wire, tourmaline, lye.

The sister text that began with
The Book of Salt, Sand & Rope.

A fly spins on a sheet of white melamine.
A fly is frozen in ice.

THE GREEN HAT, DAY 2

The sun hits the green
hat at a right angle
making shadows touch the storm
drain. It's below freezing.
My windows steam.

Someone wears a hat
like that if headed to take
care of serious business.
There are papers to be
signed, yet we wait,

God keep me from ever
completing anything.
This whole book
is but a draught—nay,
but the draught of a draught

PIERRE THE PHILOSOPHER

Let it soak;
cake your fingernails in wax.
The circular motion acts
as impediment, antidepressant.
Relax. What a quiet stampede.
What a soft way to end a parade.
A train floats over the tracks.

It's raining mushrooms, monsieur.
Her long hair arbored him in ebon vines.

The Unfettered Finn is what we
once called him.

AHAB'S LEG

Found one night lying prone
upon the ground, his ivory limb
so violently displaced,

the blade stake-wise,
and all but pierced his groin;
nor was it without

the agonizing wound
was entirely cured;
he too plainly seemed to see,

that as the most poisonous reptile
of the marsh perpetuates
his kind as inevitably as the sweetest

songster of the grove: *so, equally*
with every felicity all miserable events
do naturally beget their like

while some

natural enjoyments
here shall have
   no children

born   to them
for   the other   world,

   on the contrary   shall be followed

by
all hell's despair
  whereas some   GUILTY

mortal miseries   *shall still*

fertilely beget to

themselves

an eternally   progressive   progeny

of GRIEFS

beyond the GRAVE

not at all to hint   of this

there still seems

an inequality in the deeper

analysis of the thing

to trail genealogies

of those high   MORTAL

miseries, carries us at last

among the sourceless primogenitors

of the gods

the ineffaceable sad birth-

MARK

in the brow is the   stamp

of sorrows

speechless refuge

                   among   the marble senate

                of the DEAD

invest itself   with TERRORS

     not entirely   underived

from the land

                        of SPIRITS

and of wails

ISHMAEL

Hagar,
where have
you

come from,
where are you
going?

Behold, you
are with
child. He

shall be
a wild ass
of a man,

his hand
against every
man,

every man's
hand
against him.

FOUND LETTER

The name look-
ed familiar, blotted
out by a faint
smear. Rain. I stand
in the water,
the moving river,
silver air. Hold
it there.

II.

DEAD LETTER

I wake in the cemetery,
raise my finger
to the foggy sky & draw
a slanted mausoleum.

Place what's left of my
father's ashes inside its mauve
walls. Prop the door with my mother's
wooden leg. Carve a window

in the granite so my last
phantom has air.
Each suicide a successful
attempt at sublimation,

the gravedigger warned me.
I crawl naked
in circles on a mountain
of femur-shaped spirea.

This is what the Bible
promised. I am.
A beetle, fingers & toes
flail in the wind.

QUEEQUEG MASK

In the shed, mix creosote & cum.
Spread its thick paste across my forehead.

Light three sticks of jasmine
& inhale cords of smoke

as the tympanum rattles in my skull.
Carve this coffin from oak.

Each night outside of time, I stack
the letters on thin strips of glass.

Lie inside its contours, still,
waiting for the wind.

Listen to the harpoon:
If a man made up his mind to live,

mere sickness could not kill him.

THE GREEN HAT, DAY 3, EVENING

The TV low, we hear
muffled voices
whisper an important secret
just out of reach. I write
two notes about the green hat.

The first describes its texture:
sodden, thick, frozen;
slush damp and snowy. Skin
cells, probably hard strands
of hair trapped inside.

The owner must have green
eyes, a body that moves
in confident strides across ice
floes, oceans. A head held
high, one who never looks back—

ISHMAEL'S MIRROR

His ghost stands by the windowsill.
I see him when I close my eyes,
swallow a final drink, crush the last pill,

not believing this scene is real.
Looking, waiting, familiar disguise—
his ghost stands by the windowsill.

Every thought the same, my face is steel—
shadows from the lamp, a buzzing fly.
Swallow a final drink. Crush the last pill.

Past self hanging on: he's hard to kill.
Hold my breath; silence is the prize.
His ghost stands by the windowsill.

The sound of his voice, an unpaid bill.
Gray hair, black cloak—he looks so wise.
Swallow a final drink, crush the last pill,

write lines in my book, recite them all at will:
the words I remember most are mostly lies.
His ghost waits by the windowsill.
I swallow a final drink, crush my last pill.

SELF-PORTRAIT AS PIERRE GUYOTAT'S *ÉDEN, ÉDEN, ÉDEN*

In prison I could make myself come
without touch. Palms spread under

brown hair imagining open mouths,
sweat, salt. Sound of metal banging

against a door. Dirty, makeshift tattoo
pen hammering into some boy's

skin. Whir of the fan in a ninety-degree
night. Erection pressing through the thin

thread of blue trousers, white, piss-
marked briefs. Begin to float over

everyone sleeping in the open, my
philosophy of bent image, ontology

of existence in general population.
Closing my eyes, I see Wazzag's tarantula,

muscle twitch, semen drip down
a swollen nose, bitten lip. Smell

fluorescent cleaner, taste moss.
Imagine fellating the shadow until

thrown onto sand, cough fuming in torso;
vipers darting forth, horns catching clot.

Entering silence, coolness pricks over my
body, a wet, dark-blue center of my pants.

Opening my eyes, I see sticks floating
in the thick August air, dead branches.

ARTIST

Lucy sprays an ejaculating cock
    on the side of the water tower.
I helped, stole cans from the hard-
    ware store earlier, shoving
them in a duffel then meeting
    at the abandoned tracks
by the old middle school.
    Belly full of ants, I chew seven sticks
of Big Red, take a sniff of glue.
    Stare up at Lucy as we climb.
A red hooded sweatshirt,
    unzipped, tight black
jeans, blonde hair in a tie. Watch:
    the apprentice studies the master
deftly maneuvering legs, hands in time.
    What I thought would take
forever is over in seconds.
    Skin pressing, scrape of chapped lips.
Acetone, xylene, toluene.
    My father has been dead seven long years.
Lucy's breath is metal and cigarettes.

OHIO

Drinking Wild Turkey in a peeling
canoe, land-bound, by

the drained swimming pool.

The leaves stare as we turn
to run. Our plan is to break

the glass, swipe the fancy heirloom.

You talk me down with a shy
glance. Later, we huddle in

the flooded basement, watching

the washing machine float by.
We call it a chapel.

Then the rain. Then the snow.

The click beetles scratching at the door.
Bills in a pile by the gas stove.

I taste your dirty wine scarf;

your hands knead my stiff neck.
The snow buries the house till we can't see.

Twice I fix soup you refuse to eat.

BARTLEBY

The heft of a mountain in a keyhole.
Look at you—your head in the sky,

what will your hands be after summer,

after the rain bleeds through?
I prefer not to.

You can teach water to talk this way,

to copy names into a thick blue book.
Stare at a wall like a coffin

falling from a window.

In the office breath hovers over gray
steps, lemony ink.

See him walking with bent back.

On the cloudy ledger, flecks of torn skin.
See him chewing his watch like a leaf—

MEMNON STONE, TERROR STONE

He would like nothing better
for a headstone than this same
imposing pile—
                    It was a familiar
thing,
                    beneath the brow
of the beetlings and menacings

came the audible words of Pierre:

~

If the miseries of the undisclosable
things in me, shall ever unhorse
me from my manhood's seat; if
invisible devils do titter at us
when we most nobly strive; if
Life be a cheating dream, and Virtue
as unmeaning and unsequeled,
then do thou, Mute Massiveness,
fall on me!

~

The boughs bent and waved
to the rushes of a
                    sudden, balmy
wind; slowly Pierre crawled forth,
stood haughtily upon his feet,

as he owed thanks to none, and went
his moody way.

AMBERGRIS

Here, underwater, bubbles are bells.
Whales cathedrals
who spin in coruscating kelp
while we mimic the ribs of divers,
this one paper lantern
barreling toward
the bottom of the sea.

I chew tinfoil.
Here, in Bruges, bells
are soaked in salty brine.
I kill time.
Tiresias counts important green pebbles.
See my pus shine
behind foil-wrapped oleander.

THE GREEN HAT, DAY 4

The fat black grackles
from the cemetery hover
over the green hat. They seem
wary to land, inspect.
I can't say I blame them.

In the town's restaurant, once,
I saw a figure wearing
a green hat not unlike the one
in salt and debris
on the street. I thought

this person knows all
about culture. I wiped my hands
on the cloth napkin, ran them
through my hair, *now*
I know how it feels to be buried.

PIERRE THE OPTIMIST

Alone again, a glass violin.
So what if you're never free.

My friends are well for the moment:
they count on the head of a pin.

Collect grass clippings from
a freshly covered grave.

Hold a gray rock, as waves
soak my leather.

My music box is always open.
Come, the earth is on fire, and I am skipping

to an ethereal cantata with hints
of a cliff's edge, broken bridge—

LIQUID CHALK

I was at a bus stop
in Newark wishing
to die,
        leaning against
a falling lamppost—

Newark is nice in November;
I was on the bus
for hours; I love riding in circles
glass pressing against

my cheek

O how each person
is traveling to or from

O how each person is busy writing
the book of life—
                please, if
this is not Newark point me

someplace else
                I have been alive

for forty years and don't know

where I am going

III.

I say again he has no face.

—Herman Melville, *Moby-Dick; or, The Whale*

POETRY

Charles Kell, in his cell.
On rusty springs staring
through a square window at a distant tree,
dreaming of the wine-dark sea.
He should be taken
behind the fence & beaten.
His *léger* hand, chopped
& stowed so students
can study it as they do pig fetuses
in formaldehyde—the monster
should move no more. He wants
to be a tree. Pumpkinhead
patched with moss, a pile of dust.
Charles Kell, kill yourself.

PIERRE'S SEVERED HEAD

Staring at the light blinking blue
from frozen branches.
A wonder it still hungers
after such a separation—
propped on this abandoned rolltop desk,
stuck with black moss,
in the middle of a forgotten wood.

I talk and talk—a babble of violet.
O iron and umber;
O Great Aluminum Reef.

Dab its damp brow with a cotton swab.
Stick a bent straw between chapped lips.
Whisper Heraclitus: *After death comes*
nothing hoped for nor imagined.

There is a pyramid on the other side
where the head—some say—might be considered
a God.

The judas hole, the inmate, the marrow glowing . . .

THE GREEN HAT, DAY 5

My erection presses our frosted
windowpane. The wind
outside is fierce yet the green hat
holds ground. You come from
behind, shape your body

to my back. *I'll be right
there*, I breathe. *Let's
drive holes into our centers
where words no longer
fit.* You laugh, grow quiet.

The plants need water, the house
settles. As I turn to descend
the green hat flickers. No,
it was the last lamp
on the street, burning out—

CABIN

Last time, I lost my watch
in the hedge.
That silvery evening,
inside its four stone

walls, I sketched you,
naked, in front of the fire.
You held a glass of warm
white wine

in your cool palm.
Smoke curled around
your face, blocking
your expression.

I apologized. Later,
the story about
the young boy
who drowned in the lake

twenty years ago. How,
on certain nights, you heard
his ghost struggle. Off
in the distance,

felt his small, slick
arms clutch algae, air.
Now, alone in the middle
of the cabin, I wait.

The sky is gray, strangely lit.
My throat aches.
The skin under my chin
peels. My sore jaw throbs.

PITTSBURGH

I.

I'm writing only to tell you
about the burning truck tire at the end
of the alley, gray smoke rising
in a clear December day.

II.

Back home. My mother
and I. For the moment
she is all right.
                   She hasn't had a drink

for two days. She had to stop on the leaf-
strewn hill   not to catch her breath

but *because my legs won't work . . .*

III.

I'm thinking in symbols and I must quit.

IV.

On the third day of our return from the city
mother stayed up drinking until 3:47 a.m.

She was working on my niece's desk.
Sanding, varnishing, until it looked

just right. I lay in bed, in my child-
hood room, reading Pierre Senges'

Fragments of Lichtenberg.

V.

No one here sleeps.

Cardinals
                    plummet from the sky
toward the frozen ground.

Christmas tomorrow. Mother, sister,
niece. Each day in Ohio
is winter and more winter.

VI.

The gods have given me ears to hear,
fingers to write. But they have not
given me eyes and for this
I curse them.

VII.

No one here, anymore, dreams.
The cape of frost covers

us, the water we drink is tinged
with rust. Her hands

of foam and pebbles. Behind her
bent figure stands a line of hills.

Happiness is trees, wine, wire,
the white lies buried

in the dresser drawer.

ISHMAEL'S ARM

The skeleton dimensions
I now proceed
to set down

are copied verbatim
from my right arm,
where I had them tattooed;

as in my wild
wanderings at that period,
there was no other

secure way of preserving
such valuable statistics.
But as I was crowded

for space, and wished
the other parts
of my body to remain

a blank page
I was then composing—
at least, what untattooed

parts might remain—
I did not trouble myself
with the odd inches;

nor, indeed, should inches
at all enter into
a congenial measurement

of the whale.

CASCANDO

I.   **FOOTFALLS**

The guard orders me to strip.
Hands over a small bar of white

soap. Watches me duck
under a cold spray of water.

You work out? he asks, slight grin
on his lips. He passes me

an orange shirt, orange pants
I must reach for. My feet squeak

in rubber soles down the hall.

II. *FAILLISSANT*

Blue jeans bunched around
ankles. Shirt hangs on a hook.
Close my eyes to feel each limb
contract, hear a muffled voice
over the Macy's intercom.

Open my eyes to see
a head, waist-level,
moving back & forth in the mirror

in front of me. For a second the brown
hair looks like mine, the jagged scar
on the side of the neck.
                    A hundred
open safety pins on the dirty carpet.

III.   THE LOST ONES

Tinfoil spins on the linoleum
under shimmering fluorescent light—

      In the soft, gray evenings this is how

we'd vanish: chalk from chewed pills
stuck in our teeth,

ginger ale, two lamps throwing stale
cigarette smoke. You traced my hand

on a cardboard box,
                whispered *this is where*
our ardor lies, where art intersects.

I crushed your lips, gently kissed your forehead,
spit on the floor.

IV.   STIRRINGS STILL

In black light at the beginning
of January, in the trailer

park, buzzed on Jack Daniel's & laughing
as we scream "Parachute Woman."

The boy blows a thin brown
line off a Rolling Stones record sleeve—

Beggars Banquet—yellow-hued toilet
stuck under graffitied walls

calling us to sniff until our rusty
noses run red. Again, I'm painting him,

his skeleton-thin body beats a bead
of time on a broken amp & I stare—

V.   ILL SEEN ILL SAID

Another skin's graffiti rubbing
off on me.
                      I stood in front
of everyone & they all knew

I was guilty.
                A man

        sat in a small wooden chair,

watching

me stride back & forth. He was scared
of what I would do if left alone.

Fearing nothing & no one.

VI. IN MY CELL

Pacing bare-chested, sweat
runs down the small of my back.

Three hundred more push-ups
& then I'll jack off. Orange

shirt rolled in a ball on the metal bed.
With a long fingernail I trace

my name into the concrete wall—

VII. *BRÈVE*

Codeine, twine,
                    climb Jacob's
ladder above is air & air.

Green tetrahedron curls
from my eye, mouth full

of plaster, cellar door.

Whisper *nebenwelt* as an IV drips.
Eels dance in blue scilla.

SOBER

Lights are off & a cigarette lit.
I try to call Pierre for a visit.

Nothing. Small black
crack in the white drywall.

MY BROKEN TOOTH

The night my father died the Winter
Olympics blared from
the floating TV. They skied down
through the closed-captioned snow.
My father looked screwed, a spare
tire under the double bed.
A purple marble like a giant eye
floating above his head.
I cracked it on glass, he said.
His Ahab tattoo frowned under a dim lamp.
Chalk in a cheek to pump down the shaky jaw.
The drinker's face repeats.
Somewhere in Nagano a neon sign blinks
making the faux fur gleam.

THE GREEN HAT, DAY 6, EVENING

In the film version of Michael
Arlen's melodramatic
novel, *The Green Hat*,
Greta Garbo plays Iris Storm,
a woman of "unsavory

reputation," whose first
husband commits suicide on
their wedding night. I wish
for a cigar to smoke, a touch
of whiskey, as I stand, thinking

about viridian. Yellow
grip curling edges
of books. A cactus
knowing water. Chairs
afloat in an ocean of trees.

CHRONOMETRICALS & HOROLOGICALS

A lesson to which Pierre would appear
to be receptive. *In things terrestrial,*
a man must not be governed
by ideas celestial.

We never learn. No conclusion
of what remains. A map, a gambit.
The pamphlet offers a false dichotomy.
The effort to live in this world

is, somehow, apt to invoke
those inferior beings in strange, unique
follies and sins, unimagined before.
He walks away still clinging

to an *infallible instinct.* April.
Apathy. A deeply felt unfeeling.
Here the pages are torn
and come to a not untidy termination.

THE STOICS

False winter, suffering
without words. On the riverbank

frozen water, foot over ice.
Brittle mirror. A boy fell in last

year, branch reached out to catch
a receding hand. Over in an hour.

Mother collapsed on glass
leaves, you held her

shaking under a thick blanket.
Never a word. No sound

except pen scratching paper.
They say it was horrible to watch.

Two hours later the sky—savage clear.
Quick, quicker, quickest.

TORN LICHEN

Along the riverbank—
ghost-like, a pear
floats in the silvery air
waiting to be touched. I was hunting
again that dream of crystal
trees with leaves heavy
from the weight of green pears.
My initials carved next to yours,
deep & knotted & hard
to make out through the fog.

I closed my eyes as a painter
might before layering
initials on the canvas. Twenty
years ago, I brushed torn
lichen against your damp cheek,
watched the starving skein of ants
devour the pears. We laughed, *not
even cigarette smoke can deter
them from their task.*

Your left arm in a wine-
stained cast.
    Your eyes fixed
on a cross made from branches.

A numb wasp drooped from a twig.

I never had anyone to talk to,
you whispered, *and I know I never will.*

IV.

SOMETHING DEAD THAT DOESN'T KNOW IT'S DEAD

The blue smudge in the corner of the canvas
has a name I can't remember.
It was glued there, back in the other
Midwestern city with a name

that eludes me as well. That yellow bird
hiding in the tree, see it?
Crouch low and follow it. Barely
make a sound. Let go of the brush,

the pencil in your outstretched hand.
Pretend you are silently sliding in a field
that is, in fact, a sheet of black glass.
I have had this feeling for so long

that I'm not really here. Lapis, grosbeak,
spruce—words mean nothing to me.

PIERRE THE PESSIMIST

What is a tale told by an idiot called?
His hands tickle the harp,

watching with measured alacrity
while the world dissolves.

My little instrument, broken again,
dripping with treatment,

in search of lost time as the tired nurse
ties another bandage.

What do the stairwells on top
of stairwells mean? I feel lean in the jowl,

with a hungry look. A beetle,
almost, pink foam pearls for eyes. I rip

the book, douse each page with gasoline.
My strings—

THE GREEN HAT, DAY 7

A rat runs in small
circles where the green
hat used to lie. A stranger
with heavy hands must
have snatched it when walking by.

My eyelids feel dipped
in sand. The knocking of
the shutter shakes our white
walls. A painting falls. A door
slams. Shelves tilt like a galleon's

hull, spilling knick-knacks
over the wine-stained carpet.
Sleep, the confession
is half over. Even the judge
is weary. Nails rain down, crack

the window. The green hat

somewhere in a coal-veined sky.

PEAR TREE

We pulled the hard pears down
from the tree & smashed
them with a wooden tennis
racket until pulp stuck

to the strings & sticky green skin
matted our curly hair.
I was a sensualist then, in my youth,
tracing your yellow scabs

with an obsession.
Slowly again the salt
around the nape of your neck.
What was there in that rural

Ohio August has gone—your swift
movements in stained shorts, top
two buttons undone, how you
bit your lip after saying too much.

I bought a pear an hour ago from
the chain supermarket.
I place it on the table, watch it grow
brown. In this white January my body

starts to betray. A cabin
in the glass appears far away. Shutters
silently knock in the wind.
Tall grass pokes through the snow.

POKER

Hard to run with hands
tied behind my back.
I give a little skip—over ash,
ocean, sagebrush—to show
my defiant will.
A cloud mocks me with its opulent sway.
Weeks since I threw away my pills,
days since my last bottle, drained.

I can fly. The dregs
dance in anticipation.
A deck of cards balances bareback.
Taut rhomboids hold the queen of spades.
Wherever I turn there's my face.
A mask of gin, mask of Klonopin.
A mask built from closely watching water
watching air.

THE IDIOT

I.   DOSTOEVSKY

Staring into the spinning roulette,
bound in a suit up to my sockets.
Black, red, green spiral of smoke, a cigarette—
I left it back there, I forget
talking to my face in the wall, the devil.
Why this shiver again, this icy chill?

II. MY NAME IS CHARLES

The charred walls and damp grass of Casarsa.
Happiness, children on swings in summer.

A spider rests on my wife's hair tie,
black speck forever waiting in the mind.

Sobriety isn't teeth or a metal drill.
It is watching a movie with the blinds drawn.

It was the end of my tea with oblivion,
the children younger than I'd ever been . . .

How long before no one remembers?
There was a life that mirrored its picture—

III. *ST. JAMES AND THE MAGICIAN HERMOGENES* (1565)

He watches a face that is not really a face.
When the unclean spirit leaves man, he passes through a waterless place—
No one lights a lamp only to put it in a cellar.
Instead of a fish, a serpent; instead of air, a door.

IV.   CARRIE

I want to draw you, in your pink robe,
legs slightly open,

        gazing at the TV, my body at last
grounded with a book of Pierre Reverdy

on the coffee table. For thirteen years
I've floated in the atmosphere

        ready to burst, the brown strands
of your hair keeping me there.

All this time I've been drawing you.

OUBLIETTE

I.

He can no longer hold the guitar.
I close my eyes, see the chair, body,
black Epiphone sliding to the floor,

feel strings scratch my skin,
listen to his breath rise and fall, smile
at the white wall. Marc rests

in the recliner, slowly wasting away.
Earlier we camped in an East
Cleveland sports bar drinking, staring

at the game, front teeth numb
from cocaine. I thought about
what he asked me eight years ago.

At noon we met and I drove
him to court. The outcome OK: small
fine, costs. Later, we cruised the side

streets looking for a hole-in-the-wall.
I told myself to leave, promised my
wife. I drink, take a few drugs—

do I help or hurt? I watch
his lips curve when he says *Let's go*.
Lake Erie polluted beyond repair.

II.

The echo of the Epiphone rings,
4:00 a.m., muscle twitch, runny nose,
pounding head. The only mirror

in the apartment is a small
smudged square of glass
tilting on the bathroom sink.

What does he see when he gazes
with his one good eye—
Will you write

my obituary? You tell the truth,
will you say what I can't?
In the glass, my pale face blurs.

III.

Marc snores softly in his bed
a few feet away, the leukemia
spreading in his blood. I promised

I wouldn't write about the wreck,
say his name again. When I rise, walk
out the door—will I ever come back?

All the sidewalks are cracked.
Broken bottles and cigarette butts
on top of empty plastic bags. Tufts

of brown grass through concrete.
A siren mixed with wind.

GUILTY

I OD'd last night and was saved
by my childhood friend and his mother.
Two bottles of Narcan up my nose until
my eyes popped.

Kathy splashed cold water, Lucas punch-
slapped my chest purple:
my eyes flew open.
I ran from the ambulance, stumbled into a sea

of nasturtiums. My purple chest,
humid air cocooned in abeyance.
Running from the cops into a field,
sweating, barefoot, my toes curling warm mud.

Hot air, skin in suspension.
I willed myself awake. Iron-straight,
sweating, barefoot, nails digging into my thighs,
keeping my eyes open, sitting alone.

I willed myself into the middle of Morrison's field.
Two bottles of Narcan up my nose,
sitting alone.
I OD'd last night was I saved.

APOSTATE

In a church I crept and prayed the Song
of the Heathen. A plaster
Christ nailed with blood, thorns.
My body a severed finger.

Wasps crawled over the sugar donuts,
the pan dulce, as I stared
at my reflection in a window
at a San Miguel bakery.

A cross the size of a jacaranda leans
as men and women whispered words
I don't know. Carrie brushed my neck.
Last night I dreamt of Caravaggio

with blue lips, palm full of rotten
grapes, yellow skin. Naked—
I squeezed into a fist,
cracked a knuckle.

I was trying not to drink
and my hands shook.

MARTIN KIPPENBERGER'S BICYCLE

The pillbox, the rose, the searchlights.
The hat blows away
& the rusty chain lies taut
strangling the places that turn small
wheels.

I was dope sick once, in a strange city.
Some curious passersby stopped
& with a gold tube of lipstick
drew an outline around my shadow.
One camera snapped the infamous

image. Mere flesh, a steel box.
Framed by her vertical sarcophagus,
tiny & straight & not moving.
I—or the shape I was at this second—
crashed against my inner Id.

It was night, but not red.

FRAMES

The scene moves farther away,
while you consider the dinner tables
little archipelagoes in your anesthetic
sway, how each one   belongs
not here
            how a squiggly line forms
the shade of one eye, lashes, the charcoal
bridge of a nose, the shoulders which descend
to nothing.

For the moment we are floating
            out on one of the black
islands you describe so clearly, *serene*
            comfort, you say,
though your eyes bore into me a lightning
            not unlike a rusty cattle prod.

One thinks of all the innocent, harmed somewhere,
            mutilated beyond recognition.
Frozen horror trapped on their faces.
I count how you used to come to me,
            curl in a ball, pressing against.
How you recalled your dreams over morning coffee.
How you described each month as if it were a color.

How I took you to the hospital.
November, you say. I forget
why. January orange. July,
the month you hated most, pink.

How the last time you drove yourself, while
I stayed behind, staring into a forest
from the window. Waiting, a reminder, that one can draw
loss, draw frost without anyone knowing

what it is, draw the color of night, draw—
for the final time—the light reaching the trees into nowhere.

AMERIKA

Kafka is somewhere in Kansas,
in a field, letting dirt sift
through his outstretched fingers.
He prays for a fox

to break the corn stalks,
a cool stream suddenly to appear.
I plan to rent a gray sedan
and go looking for him.

I will bring the bees
asleep in a white box.
A copy of Ovid.
I know the song by heart,

the one cardinals sing in November,
before the snow falls.
We might rob a bank or sit
on the edge of some cliff

pondering the vast void.
The circus will be in full swing,
we will sip a wine
made to taste like fresh grasses.

CHALK

I juggle sea glass again.
Count the cadence of the wind
as it whistles through the hole
in the window.
Try to avoid my reflection—

impossible—how one eye
catches, a second too long.
Glance—shadow. A quick flick.
The house shakes, a wine glass vibrates.
As a child I ran barefoot

through the tall, uncut grass
pretending it was the ocean,
stomped unaware on a wasp hive
that had fallen from a linden,
felt the cool, feathery paper

under my heel until the sharp & needles.
The sky fell—I tasted chalk.
Copies of Twombly,
erratic circles, stream
on a canvas, scrawled pastels.

I was swimming underwater.
Broken pieces, failed.
A man who must have been my father
stood there, mother—far off.
In a white room,

triangles on the wall tried to speak
from my steel-wool-mouth.
I saw my face reflected from a metal
cup—black circles where my eyes
should be—open, dark.

NOTES

"The Green Hat, Day 2" includes lines from chapter 32, "Cetology," from Herman Melville's *Moby-Dick; or, The Whale* (1851).

"Ahab's Leg" includes lines from chapter 106, "Ahab's Leg," from *Moby-Dick*.

"Ishmael" includes lines from Genesis, from the revised standard version of the Bible.

"Queequeg Mask" includes lines from chapter 110, "Queequeg in His Coffin," from *Moby-Dick*.

"Self-Portrait as Pierre Guyotat's *Éden, Éden, Éden*" includes lines from Pierre Guyotat's *Éden, Éden, Éden* (1970; trans. Graham Fox, 1995).

"Bartleby" includes the famous line "I prefer not to" from Herman Melville's "Bartleby, the Scrivener: A Story of Wall-Street" (1853).

"Memnon Stone, Terror Stone" includes lines from Book VII, "Intermediate between Pierre's Two Interviews with Isabel at the Farm-house," from Herman Melville's *Pierre; or, The Ambiguities* (1852).

"Pierre's Severed Head" includes lines from *Fragments: The Collected Wisdom of Heraclitus* (trans. Brooks Haxton, 2001).

"Ishmael's Arm" includes the last paragraph from chapter 102, "A Bower in the Arsacides," from *Moby-Dick*.

"Chronometricals & Horologicals" includes lines from Book XIV, "The Journey and the Pamphlet," from *Pierre* and David Faflik's *Melville and the Question of Meaning* (2018).

Section II, "My Name Is Charles," from "*The Idiot*" is influenced by Donald Revell's "My Name Is Donald," from *The Bitter Withy* (2009), and contains a few words from Pier Paolo Pasolini's poem, "My Former Life," from *The Selected Poetry of Pier Paolo Pasolini* (trans. Stephen Sartarelli, 2014).

ACKNOWLEDGMENTS

Grateful acknowledgment is made to the journals where some of these poems first appeared:

Abstract; *Asheville Poetry Review*; *Atlanta Review*; *Blood Tree Literature*; *Bluestem*; *The Brooklyn Review*; *Collider*; *DASH*; *Fauxmoir*; *filling Station*; *The Florida Review*; *Ghost Proposal*; *Hobart*; *The Ilanot Review*; *Kestrel*; *Laurel Review*; *Layman's Way*; *LIGEIA*; *MAYDAY*; *The Maynard*; *Miracle Monocle*; *Quiddity*; *Rust + Moth*; *SurVision*; *Temenos*; *Thin Air*; *Treehouse*; and *Up North Lit*.

Some poems appear in *Pierre Mask* (2021), one of SurVision Books' 2019 James Tate Chapbook Prize winners.

My thanks to Miguel Murphy for friendship, for time, for all the help with this book. It wouldn't exist without you.

Thanks, once again, to Christine Stroud for all the invaluable care and attention.

My deep gratitude to Donald Revell for kindness, thoughtfulness, and encouraging words.

My sincere thanks to Susan Stewart for kind words and for helpful feedback.

Thank you, Vi Khi Nao, for your words, your generosity.

Thank you, Steve Langan. Reading and rereading your magical book, *Freezing* (2001), helped me through a difficult spell in 2017. The "Green Hat" poems are an homage and they are for you.

Thank you, Peter Covino. Thank you, Timothy Liu.

My thanks also to Sandra Kell, Lisa Galati, Marcus Tirabasso, Brandi George, Mike Good, Devan Murphy, Jon Riccio, David Faflik, Kenneth Salzer, and Lucas Morrison.

My wife, Carrie—all my love for you, none of this without you.

NEW AND FORTHCOMING

The Scorpion's Question Mark by J. D. Debris
Winner of the 2022 Donald Justice Poetry Prize,
selected by Cornelius Eady

Given by Liza Katz Duncan
Winner of the 2022 Rising Writer Prize in Poetry,
selected by Donika Kelly

Origami Dogs: Stories by Noley Reid

Taking to Water by Jennifer Conlon
Winner of the 2022 Autumn House Poetry Prize,
selected by Carl Phillips

The Neorealist in Winter: Stories by Salvatore Pane
Winner of the 2022 Autumn House Fiction Prize,
selected by Venita Blackburn

Discordant by Richard Hamilton
Winner of the 2022 CAAPP Book Prize,
selected by Evie Shockley

Otherwise: Essays by Julie Marie Wade
Winner of the 2022 Autumn House Nonfiction Prize,
selected by Lia Purpura